close to the batsman in front of the wicket. Here quick reactions are crucial, as is a degree of bravery.

2. Ring fielders

This includes fielding positions such as cover point, square leg and extra cover. They are often called ring fielders as in a one-day game they would field inside the 30-metre ring. The main job of ring fielders is to stop the batsmen taking

This is an outstanding slip catch. Notice how the fielder is keeping his eyes on the ball.

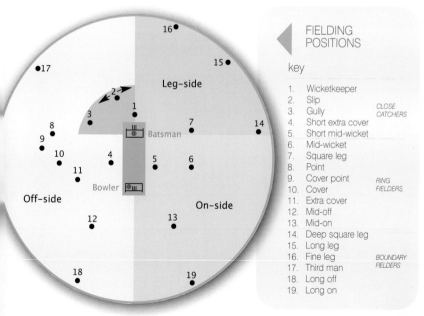

FIELDING POSITIONS

key

1.	Wicketkeeper	
2.	Slip	CLOSE
3.	Gully	CATCHERS
4.	Short extra cover	
5.	Short mid-wicket	
6.	Mid-wicket	
7.	Square leg	
8.	Point	
9.	Cover point	RING
10.	Cover	FIELDERS
11.	Extra cover	
12.	Mid-off	
13.	Mid-on	
14.	Deep square leg	
15.	Long leg	
16.	Fine leg	BOUNDARY
17.	Third man	FIELDERS
18.	Long off	
19.	Long on	

Diagram labels: 16, 15, 17, Leg-side, 2, 1, 3, 7, 14, Batsman, 8, 9, 10, 4, 5, 6, 11, Bowler, Off-side, On-side, 12, 13, 18, 19

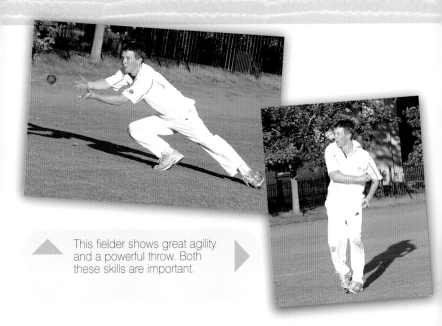

This fielder shows great agility and a powerful throw. Both these skills are important.

singles and to try to get a run out. They will also be called on to stop fiercely struck shots that are heading toward the boundary and to take catches. Great fielders in these positons must be quick, agile, able to anticipate where the ball is going, and have good hands and an accurate throw. Australia's Michael Clarke and England's Paul Collingwood are brilliant in these areas.

3. Boundary fielders

Boundary fielders field out in the deep. Their job is to try and stop the ball going for four or six. They will also be required to take high catches when big hits are mis-timed. To be a good boundary fielder you must have be fast, agile and have a powerful throw. Australia's Andrew Symonds is one of the best in the world in this position.

BACKING UP

In any piece of fielding at least three players will be involved. One person fields the ball while a second, usually the wicketkeeper or the bowler, will be at the stumps to receive the throw. It is vital that a third player 'backs up' by getting in position beyond the stumps to intercept the throw if the receiver misses. Good fielding teams will automatically back up at both ends.

About the author

Luke Sellers is an ECB-qualified coach. He is the community cricket coach for Gloucestershire, working with young players of all abilities and in coach education.

England's James Anderson makes a spectacular stop off his own bowling during a one-day international.

INTRODUCTION

Whatever your special skill – bowler, batsman or all-rounder – you will spend more time fielding than doing anything else in a normal cricket match. Therefore it is vital to master and enjoy it.

A good fielder will be quick and agile, have a strong, accurate throw and be a good catcher. The old saying 'catches win matches' is a favourite among coaches and commentators alike, and underlines the importance of a safe pair of hands in the field. With the increasing amount of one-day cricket, fielding is more important than ever before. A good fielder, such as England ace Paul Collingwood, can save many runs in a game for his team.

FIELDING POSITIONS

There are many different fielding positions and each one will require a slightly different set of skills. We can divide fielding positions into three main types.

WHAT MAKES A GOOD FIELDER?

- Powerful, accurate throw
- Good catching ability
- Speed
- Agility
- Anticipation and awareness
- Concentration
- Bravery

1. Close catchers

This includes positions such as slip, gully and short-leg. If you are fielding close to the wicket your main job is to take a catch if a chance comes your way. The ball will normally come to you in the air and often very quickly. To field here you must have good hands, quick reactions, bravery, anticipation and concentration. Top slip fielders, such as England's Andrew Flintoff or South Africa's Graeme Smith, are able to react in a split second to balls flying off the edge of the bat to take crucial catches for their team. Great close fielders such as Australia's Mike Hussey often field

THE READY **POSITION**

The ready position is a crucial part of preparation for all fielders other than close catchers. This is the movement made just before the bowler releases the ball, and it should put fielders in a balanced, athletic position from which they can move in any direction.

GETTING READY

The ready position has similarities with a football goalkeeper or a tennis player at the net. The fielder will be able to react quickly and deter the batsman from taking a single.

COACHING POINTS

- As the bowler runs in, start to walk towards the striker's end.

- Make sure you are light on your feet and in a slightly crouched position with your head still and your eyes level.

- Just before the bowler releases the ball make a small jump that puts you in a balanced, athletic position on the balls of your feet.

- You should be looking at the batsman and be prepared to react quickly once the ball is struck.

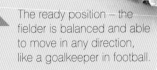

The ready position – the fielder is balanced and able to move in any direction, like a goalkeeper in football.

CLOSE **CATCHING**

Close catchers are fielders who stand in positions such as slip, gully or short leg. They field close to the wicket to try to catch the batsman out. Fielders in these positions must have a safe pair of hands and fast reactions. They must also be able to concentrate for long periods of time.

BE THE BEST

Improve your reactions by using different balls, such as a toy rubber bouncy ball. Practise bouncing it against an upturned paving slab or wall and see how quickly it flies back. This will really test those reactions.

COACHING POINTS

Stance: You should be comfortable and balanced in your stance, ready to move left, right, high or low depending on where the ball comes.

• Feet should be at least shoulder-width apart with your weight on the balls of your feet.
• Knees should be slightly flexed.

Close catchers should make sure they are well balanced and watch the ball right into their hands.

 To be a top fielder you also need to be an athlete. Sri Lanka's Jehan Mubarek is at full stretch to pull off a brilliant catch in a Test match against India.

- Your hands should be together, fingers pointing at the ground, at roughly knee height.
- You must keep your head up and eyes level at all times.

Catching:

- Watch the ball all the way into your hands.
- Give with your hands as you take the ball, bringing them towards your body.
- Always use two hands where possible.
- If the catch is below waist height always take the ball with your fingers pointing down.
- Keep your head over the ball.

Practice

Work with a partner 3 to 5 metres away, throwing the ball underarm to each other, below waist height. This will help you to get the right technique before you increase the difficulty of the practice. Once you start to feel confident you can vary the speed, height and direction of the throw.

You can practise close catching on your own by throwing a tennis ball underarm against a wall. Use an old, uneven stone wall, as the ball will bounce off at unpredictable angles, which sharpens your reactions.

CATCHING IN THE **DEEP**

If you are fielding on the boundary you may have to take a high catch from an attempted big hit from the batsman. There are two ways of taking a high catch – the orthodox method and the reverse cup – and you should practise both. Go for the one that feels most comfortable, but whichever method you use it is important to stay balanced and get your hands into position quickly.

ORTHODOX METHOD

- Move underneath the ball as quickly as possible, keeping your head steady.
- Feet should be at least shoulder-width apart so you are in a balanced position, with your knees slightly bent.
- Bring your hands together and spread your fingers, with your little fingers together, parallel to the ground.
- Take the catch at eye level or above.

GO FOR IT!

Relax your hands as you take the ball, and it will be less likely to bounce out.

- Close your hands around the ball and 'give', bringing the ball in to your chest.

Common fault

Some players try and take a high catch with their fingers pointing upwards. This can lead to injury if the ball catches the top of your finger, so keep your fingers parallel to the ground.

REVERSE CUP METHOD

- Move into position as you would for catching by the orthodox method.
- Reverse your hands so your fingers point up with your palms facing the ball (see picture 2, opposite). Your thumbs should be together or crossed over.

- Watch the ball all the way into your hands.
- Take the catch at eye level or above.
- As you take the ball, 'give' with your hands and bring the ball in towards your shoulder.

Practice

You can practise high catching on your own by simply throwing the ball up vertically, underarm and a little in front of you, and then moving to take the catch. Try both methods of high catch so you are comfortable using either.

A fun practice to try if you have a partner or team mates around is to mark out three evenly sized areas A, B and X. One player/team stands in area A, the other in area B. Area X is left empty.

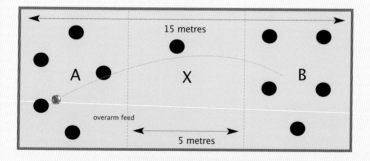

A player in team A throws the ball underarm over area X, trying to land it in team B's territory. A fielder in team B takes the catch and tries to land the ball in area A. Points are awarded if a team lands the ball in the opposing area and are deducted if the throwing side lands the ball in zone X.

Next step

The game can be made harder by making the areas bigger and by using more than one ball.

THE SKIM CATCH

The reverse cup method is used for taking a 'skim' catch between chest and head height when the ball is travelling towards you on a flat trajectory. You might use this type of catch if fielding at point or cover. You may need to bend your knees to get into position.

Practice

A good way to practise the skim catch is by using a tennis racquet and tennis ball. Stand about 15 metres away from the person with the racquet, who should aim to hit a flat shot that reaches the catcher at head height. Start by getting the hitter to hit the ball

fairly gently, then build up the speed. You can also get him to hit the ball to either side of you once you have gained confidence.

The reverse cup method is used to take a skim catch.

OVERARM **THROW**

A powerful overarm throw is essential for any top fielder, whether you are in the deep trying to save runs or going for a run out from the in-field. England all-rounder Andrew Flintoff has such a strong arm that he can throw the ball accurately to the top of the stumps from any boundary in the world.

COACHING POINTS

- Make sure you hold the ball across the seam. If you hold the ball with a vertical seam it may swing after release and you will lose accuracy.
- Take a long, straight stride to ensure you are balanced and have a firm 'base'. Your back foot should be at 90 degrees to the target. If you are right-handed you will have your left leg nearest the target, right leg for left-handers.
- Point your front arm at the target and pull back your throwing arm.

India's Rohan Gavaskar throws from a wide base and uses his front arm to point at the target.

- Make an L shape with your throwing arm, ensuring the elbow is level or above your shoulder. Turn chest-on to the target so your hips and shoulders start to open.
- As your chest faces the target drive your front arm forward and release the ball with your front leg bent.
- The upper body completes a half-turn. Drag your back leg forward and brace your front leg.
- Your front arm should follow through, passing across your body and finishing by your opposite hip.
- It is important to keep your head still and eyes level, looking at the target throughout the movement.

Common fault

Many players throw with the elbow of the throwing arm lower than their shoulder. This can lead to injury.

Practice

It can be difficult to put all the movements of the overarm

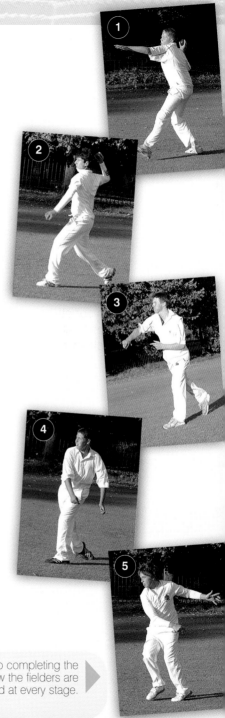

From taking aim to completing the throw, notice how the fielders are balanced at every stage.

throw together, so break it down at first. Your 'throwing leg' is the same side as your throwing arm.

1. Start by practising the wrist flick. Kneel on your throwing leg 3 metres from your target and grip the wrist of your throwing arm with your other hand. With your arm in an upright position flick your wrist and fingers and bounce the ball towards the target.

2. Move on to the elbow flick. This time kneel 5 metres from the target and grip your upper arm just below the elbow. Flick your elbow, wrist and fingers to bounce the ball towards the target.

3. Next, kneel 10 metres from your target. Start with your throwing arm in an L shape with a high elbow. After release complete a full follow through so your throwing arm comes across your body.

4. Now try it standing up.

THROWING AT THE STUMPS

When you feel confident with your throwing you can put it into a game with just one other person or in small teams. Place two sets of stumps side by side in the middle of the two players. Each player must be at least 10 metres away from the stumps. Take it in turns to throw overarm at the stumps. Give yourself 10 points for hitting the target and 2 points if you field the ball cleanly from your opponent's throw. The winner is the player with the most points. To make it harder you can remove one set of stumps or increase the distance from which you throw.

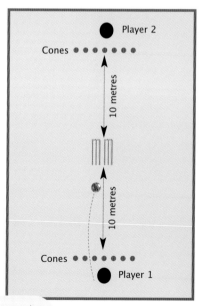

This is a good practice to increase the accuracy of your throw.

ONE-HANDED **INTERCEPT**

This is a fast, attacking fielding skill used by fielders in the ring, such as cover or mid-wicket, when the batsman has pushed the ball into the in-field and is looking to take a quick single. The fielders' job is to stop the batsman attempting the run, or to run them out if they have already set off. It is important to be quick off the mark and to throw the ball in as soon as possible.

COACHING POINTS

- Attack the ball at speed in a balanced position, low to the ground.
- Pick the ball up outside your throwing foot with your fingers pointing down and your palm facing the ball (see picture 1).

- Staying low, move your head up to look at the target. As your throwing arm completes its backswing, point your non-throwing arm at the target.
- After release keep your throwing arm and body moving towards the target (see picture 2).

Practice

You can practise this skill in pairs with one person as wicketkeeper, rolling the ball out and the other player as the fielder. This is a good practice to get the technique right before stepping up the speed.

Next step

A really fun drill that replicates match conditions is to include a batsman running between the wickets at the same time. Set up two groups as shown in the diagram. When the coach or wicketkeeper shouts 'go' the batsman must run, touch the cone with his/her bat and sprint

BE THE BEST

Aim to hit the stumps or throw just above the bails into the hands of the wicketkeeper.

back again. At the same time the fielder races out, runs around the stumps and completes a one-handed throw and intercept as they return. The wicketkeeper should roll the ball out just as the fielder turns. If the batsman gets back to the crease before the wicketkeeper has the ball the batting team gets a point. If the wicketkeeper receives the ball before the batsman gets back then the fielding side gets a point.

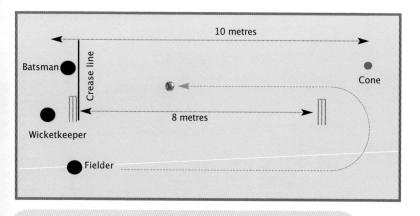

This drill is a race between two players. The batsman must touch the cone and get back to his crease before the fielder returns the ball.

The two-handed intercept is usually used when you are attacking a fiercely struck shot in the outfield. It is a quicker, more attacking method than the long barrier (see page 22) but still gives you a second line of defence in case the ball should deviate, as your throwing foot will be behind your hand. Most top fielders will combine this skill with the crow hop (see page 18) to ensure they can perform at pace and establish a good base from which to throw.

COACHING POINTS

- Approach the ball at speed at a line slightly to the non-throwing side of the ball.
- As you approach, start to lower your body, making sure you stay balanced.
- As you prepare to pick up the ball, slightly turn your non-throwing hip and shoulder towards it.
- Turn your throwing foot so that the instep is in line with the ball. Watch the ball carefully and pick it up with two hands in front of your throwing foot.
- Establish a throwing position by taking a stride with your non-throwing leg towards your target or by performing the crow hop.

Common fault

Many young players wait for the ball to come to them. This often gives the batsman a chance of an extra run. Make sure you attack the ball, approaching it at

When attacking the ball, at pace, get low to the ground and stay balanced to ensure you can pick it up cleanly.

speed. If you have your foot in the correct position this will stop the ball should you miss it with your hands. This gives you the chance to run on to the ball and perform the skill at pace.

Practice

As with the other fielding practices, the two-handed intercept drill can be practised with one other person or in two groups like a relay race. Make sure that the thrower is at least 20 metres away so that the practice is safe and the throw is used over a distance similar to that in a match.

This fielder is using the crow hop to get into position to throw the ball in quickly.

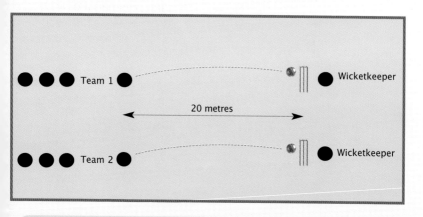

The wicketkeepers roll out the ball at the same time. Fielders must use the two-handed intercept and return the ball to the wicketkeeper. The first player to do so gets one point for their team. Repeat for each player in the team.

CROW **HOP**

The crow hop is a fielding skill that is used to get you in position to make a long, powerful throw. It is most commonly used when attacking the ball in the deep. It is a quick, effective movement that makes use of your body's momentum.

COACHING POINTS

- Approach the ball as for the two-handed intercept.
- Pick the ball up in between your feet, in front of your throwing foot with your non-throwing side nearest the target.
- As you start to stand taller bring your throwing foot behind your non-throwing foot, performing the crow hop. (You can bring your throwing foot in front of your non-throwing foot instead if it feels more comfortable.)
- Take a stride forward with your non-throwing foot to establish a strong base from which to throw.

GO FOR IT!

To perform a fast, effective crow hop attack the ball at speed and stay light on your feet.

PRACTICE

To practise the crow hop simply use it in combination with other fielding skills, such as the two-handed intercept and throw, or the long barrier.

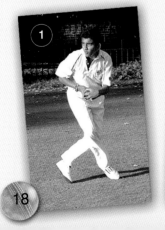

See how the fielder uses the crow hop (picture 1) to establish a good throwing position (picture 2).

RETRIEVING THE **BALL**

The retrieve is used in a game when the ball has been hit past a fielder, who then has to turn and chase it. You need to be quick on your feet and take as little time as possible between picking the ball up and throwing it in, as it could be the difference between a batsman being safe or run out. There are two types of retrieve, the short retrieve and the long retrieve.

THE SHORT RETRIEVE

- As the ball is struck past you, turn facing the ball and chase it on a line slightly to the non-throwing side of the ball (left-side for right arm throwers, right for left handers).
- As you near the ball start to lower your body.
- Slightly overrun the ball and pick up in your throwing hand, just outside your throwing foot.
- Take the weight on your throwing leg and push yourself back towards your target.
- Establish a firm base by stepping towards the target with your non-throwing foot.

Notice the player picks up the ball outside his throwing foot.

- Complete the overarm throw by returning the ball to whichever end is necessary.

Common fault

Players often try to throw the ball in before they have established a good throwing position. Make sure you are balanced before throwing to ensure maximum power and accuracy.

THE LONG RETRIEVE

There are two ways of performing the long retrieve. The first may be more effective when retrieving a slow-moving ball and the second may be easier to perform if the ball is moving at speed. Try both methods so that you are able to use either in a match if required.

Method 1

- Approach the ball in a line directly behind it.
- Lower your body towards the ground as you get nearer to the ball.
- Pick the ball up next to the instep of your non-throwing foot.
- Push yourself back towards your target with your non-throwing foot and then pivot on your throwing foot to complete the turn back towards play.
- Establish your throwing position and throw to the appropriate end.

Method 2

- Repeat the process as for method 1 to the point where you pick up the ball.

TEAMWORK

Fielders can save valuable time when retrieving the ball by working as a pair, as shown in the photographs.
The first fielder to reach the ball flicks it back to his colleague rather than turning to throw. Fielder number two is in a better position to throw the ball in quickly as he is already upright and balanced. Good communication between the fielders is vital.

• Take as few strides as possible to slow down before turning back towards the target.
• Create a wide base and complete the overarm throw.

Practice

For this practice you will need to be in pairs. One player rolls the ball out for the fielder to chase and retrieve. Have five goes and then swap roles.

If you have several players, form two groups and perform the practice as a relay race, with players in each team taking it in turns until everyone has had two goes at retrieving. By making the practice into a race you simulate the pressure of a match.

The first fielder retrieves the ball...

...and flicks it back to his team-mate...

...who throws it to the wicketkeeper.

THE LONG **BARRIER**

The long barrier is a defensive fielding skill you might use when the ball has been struck hard along the ground or on a particularly rough or bumpy outfield. It provides a second line of defence to stop the ball in case of uneven bounce.

COACHING POINTS

- Approach the ball in a low, crouched position, staying balanced.
- As you near the ball turn your non-throwing shoulder and leading hip slightly towards the ball, staying low as you do so.
- Form a long barrier at 90 degrees to the ball by placing your non-throwing knee on the ground with your throwing foot at 90 degrees to the ball.
- Pick the ball up underneath your eyes with fingers pointing down and hands together.
- Stand up and move into an overarm throwing position.

Common fault

Young players often do the long barrier the wrong way round so that their throwing leg is on the ground. This means you will have to make a big movement to get into a throwing position. Taking this extra time could cost you a run-out chance.

Practice

Practise in pairs, 10 metres apart with one person rolling the ball out and the other person performing the skill. Once you feel more confident you can get your partner to vary the pace and direction of the feed to test you a bit more.

A good team practice is to have two teams facing each other about 10 metres apart. Each team is defending a goal area. Teams take it in turns to roll the ball, trying to score in the opposite goal. The defending team must perform the long barrier to stop a goal being scored.

Notice how the fielder's leg provides a second line of defence, in case the ball takes a bad bounce.

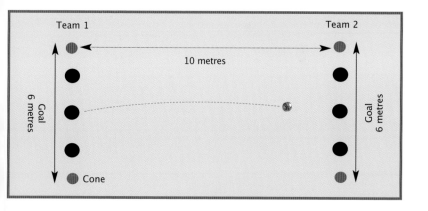

To make the practice harder you can make the goals bigger, or shorten the distance between them.

WICKETKEEPING **SKILLS**

Being a wicketkeeper is a tough but crucial job. A wicketkeeper is always in the thick of the action and must have great concentration as well as good agility and safe hands. You might go for long periods without any chances coming your way and then be called upon to take a vital catch or stumping that could change the outcome of the match. As a wicketkeeper you must be comfortable against fast bowlers and standing up to the stumps against the spinners. Wicketkeepers must be able to read the type of ball being bowled and work out whether it will spin, swing, bounce or keep low. It is also the wicketkeeper's job to keep his fellow fielders focused, offering encouragement and showing energy and enthusiasm.

WHAT MAKES A GOOD WICKETKEEPER?

- A safe pair of hands
- Quick reactions
- Agility
- Speed
- Concentration
- Balance
- Ability to read the game
- Energy

To be a good wicketkeeper you must be physically fit. A wicketkeeper is always in the thick of the action and doesn't get a chance to take a breather, so good stamina and flexibility are essential. He must be comfortable catching with either hand, diving to right or left, and have quick reactions. A wicketkeeper also needs a good understanding of the game.

A wicketkeeper must be able to read how much a ball will move and learn the different variations of each bowler, such as a leg spinner's googly or a fast bowler's slower ball. Often the captain will ask the keeper for advice about field settings or how best to get a particular batsman out.

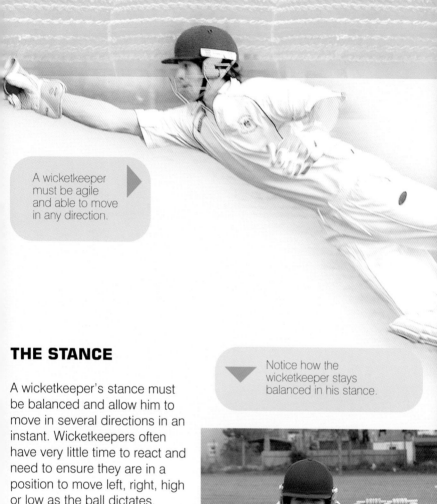

A wicketkeeper must be agile and able to move in any direction.

THE STANCE

A wicketkeeper's stance must be balanced and allow him to move in several directions in an instant. Wicketkeepers often have very little time to react and need to ensure they are in a position to move left, right, high or low as the ball dictates.

Notice how the wicketkeeper stays balanced in his stance.

- Your weight should be on the balls of your feet.
- Your hands should be together and relaxed.

The basic stance is nearly identical for standing back to seam bowlers or up to slow bowlers. The only minor change you might make is to ensure you are in a slightly lower position when standing up to the wicket.

When you are standing up it is vital that no part of your body or equipment is in front of the stumps otherwise a no ball will be called.

The stance also needs to be comfortable as keepers can spend long periods of time crouched behind the stumps.

COACHING POINTS

- Crouch slightly to the off-side of the batsman.

 The wicketkeeper is leaning slightly forward with his weight on the balls of his feet.

Top wicketkeepers are not only comfortable standing back against quick bowlers but are also superb when standing up against spin or medium pace. Standing up is a tough skill and can often separate a good keeper from a great one. India's Mahendra Dhoni is able to place real pressure on the batsman with his safe hands and lightning fast reactions when standing up to the stumps.

TAKING THE BALL

Straight

Start from the basic stance, slightly lower than when standing back.

- Keep your head and body behind the ball.
- Bring your body up with the bounce of the ball.
- Watch the ball into your hands, taking it underneath your eyes.
- If the ball has bounced below waist-height take it with your fingers pointing down and your hands in front of your body.
- Give slightly with your hands as the ball enters the gloves.

Watch the ball right into your hands.

Keep your head over the ball as you move to take it outside off stump.

Off-side take

- Move your outside foot and body towards the line of the ball.
- Try and leave your inside leg where it is, but go on to your

toes if necessary to help you reach the ball.

- Your hands should move towards the line of the ball in a low position, before coming up to take the ball with the bounce. This is called the 'L' as the journey of your hands resembles the letter L.
- Rise with the ball and watch it into your hands.
- Give with your hands as the ball enters your gloves.

Leg-side take

The leg-side take is the same as for the off-side take except the movement will be made with your inside leg.

BE THE BEST

By keeping your inside leg (off-side take) and outside leg (leg-side take) close to the stumps you will be able to push back towards the stumps quickly. This is vital when going for a stumping.

To take the ball down the leg-side move your inside leg across.

Common fault

Many young keepers bring their hands up before moving across to the ball. This means that if the ball keeps low or catches a bottom edge it will be very difficult to get your hands down in time. By bringing your hands across in a low position and using the 'L' technique you should be in a position to react. Remember, it is easier to bring your hands up to the ball then drop them down.

Practice

• Start off in your stance with a feeder about a pitch length from the stumps.

• The feeder throws the ball overarm to an area about 3 metres from the stumps to imitate a good length delivery. Throw to the off-side until the wicketkeeper is confident then switch to the leg-side.

• Finally, alternate the throws at random so the wicketkeeper has to react to the ball.

DID YOU KNOW?

Les Ames of Kent holds the record for the most stumpings in first-class cricket. He claimed 417 victims in a career lasting 25 years.

HIGH TAKE

If you are standing up to the wicket you will need to be able to take a high bouncing ball. This is particularly important if you intend to stand up to medium pace bowlers. While many of the basic points remain the same there are a few important differences.

COACHING POINTS

- Start in the basic stance.
- Move your outside leg (off-side take) or inside leg (leg-side take) back and towards the line of the ball at a 45-degree angle to the stumps.
- Twist your head and body in the direction you are moving to take the ball on the outside of your body. This is known as the 'K' method because if you were to draw lines from the crease at 45 degree angles towards the off- and leg-side it would resemble the letter 'K'.
- Rise with the bounce of the ball and give with your hands.

Common fault

Some wicketkeepers try and take the ball front on, without twisting their body. If you do this your hands will end up in an awkward position with no room to move back, making it very hard to take the ball cleanly.

Notice how the wicketkeepers body forms the K shape when taking a high ball.

Practice

Practise the same way as shown for a good length take, but ensure the feeder throws the ball shorter, so that it bounces higher.

Next step

Distract the keeper as he takes the ball by a batsman standing in front of the stumps. He should play close to the ball without making contact as it goes through.

Wicketkeepers have to be competent when standing back to seam bowlers as well as when standing up to the wicket. Top wicketkeepers in Test matches have to keep wicket to 90mph fast bowlers. This takes good footwork and quick reactions. Not only do they need a safe pair of hands, they need to be outstanding athletes as well.

COACHING POINTS

Start from the basic stance, ensuring you have a clear sight of the bowler and are standing far enough back for the ball to be taken comfortably as it starts to drop.

- **Straight:** Move into position quickly and catch the ball with your body behind it and with your head over the ball. Hands 'give' as you take the ball.
- **Off-side:** Move your feet and body across to the off-side using a side step. Make sure your weight is on the balls of your feet. Get your head in line with the ball and keep your hands low. Rise with the bounce of the ball. Hands 'give' as the ball enters your gloves.

- **Leg-side:** The coaching points for the leg-side take are the same as for the off, except you move towards the leg-side.
- **Diving:** Occasionally it may be necessary to dive for a wide delivery or a ball that has caught the edge of the bat.

The diving wicketkeeper rolls on landing to ensure he does not drop the ball.

BE THE BEST

When taking the ball two-handed keep your hands together. For a low take your fingers should point at the ground. For a high take your fingers should be parallel to the ground or your hands reversed.

- Try to dive as flat as possible.
- Try and catch the ball as late as possible to give you the best chance of reaching it.
- Roll on landing to avoid injury and jarring. If you hit the ground with a big impact there is also a chance that this may cause you to drop the ball.

Practice

The same practices suggested for standing up to the stumps can be adapted to practise standing back.

- Place two cones like a goal, about 6 metres apart. The wicketkeeper stands in the middle of this area with a feeder standing opposite 5 metres away.
- The feeder throws the ball underarm to each cone alternately. The wicketkeeper has to move across using a side step to take the ball and return it to the feeder. Throws should be about waist height and slow enough for the keeper to reach without diving.
- When the wicketkeeper is confident with this drill the feeder can throw the ball to the cones at random and also vary the height and speed of the feeds. This practice is good for learning how to move quickly on the balls of your feet while staying balanced.

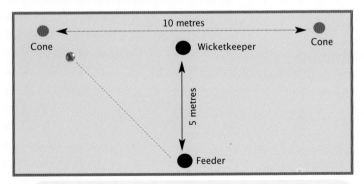

Practise standing back with this two-player drill.